2016

In loving memory of our parents

Thank you for your interest.

Gudrun Honig - Shrimpton

Gudrun Honig

PART ONE

As arranged with my husband-to-be, I returned to Canada from the United States in the middle of November. The bus had stopped at the border. "Young lady, where do you think you are going?" said the elderly passport officer at the Canadian border. I explained to him that I was returning to Canada from Los Angeles, where I had worked for six months. To my amazement the answer was, "Oh no, you are not. You cannot return to Canada: you have to re-immigrate". Suddenly my dream of living happily with my prince became a nightmare. I knew how long it takes to obtain a visa to immigrate anywhere. I also saw my prince being taken away from me by a beautiful blue-eyed blonde like my sister. I started to sob and soon could not stop the tears running down my face. The passport officer watched me closely and asked me to open my big trunk that the bus driver had dropped off. "What have you got in it?" On top lay my short wedding dress. I had bought the dress in Los Angeles at a sale, I explained to this elderly law enforcement officer. To my amazement the officer said to me after a while: "What I do now, young lady, is strictly against the law. I will let you pass." The officer had barely finished saying that when suddenly there stood before me not a Canadian immigration official, but a fairy.

Now, dear reader, not even the Brothers Grimm, who had collected the famous folk tales, in which princes, young maidens and children encountered all kinds of characters in the most unlikely circumstances, had there ever appeared a male fairy. However, here at the Canadian border, which I had to cross to get to my prince, I met one. Yet, I had no time to lose. It was essential to hurry to get away in case the fairy changed his mind. I collapsed on the bus seat and cried, but this time with relief. I decided from now on to leave behind the Brothers Grimm fairy tales of my childhood, because I had come to the end of my

Getting to know you, getting to know all about you?

Journey: I will be reunited with my prince and saw myself "living happily ever after".

Yet as I was walking down the long aisle towards the altar of Holy Rosary Cathedral in Vancouver on December 31, 1960, I started to have my doubts because of our different backgrounds. Had I made the right decision in marrying David so quickly?" He was tall, had grey eyes, big ears and was left-handed. He led an active life: skiing, sailing, and mountain climbing with the Youth Hostel people. The question on my mind was, would he be able to settle down and help me raise our children?

Gudrun Honig

Father Mallon, a young priest at the cathedral, had given David religious instructions in the Catholic faith. After I arrived back for Los Angeles, I joined for the marriage preparation's instructions. He was about the same age as us. He confessed that when he was called to the terrible accident of the 1957 collapse of the unfinished new Second Narrows Bridge (now called Iron Workers Memorial Bridge), to give the last rites to the injured and dying, he became sick to his stomach at the sight of the entangled bodies. He was like a friend to us by now. To our surprise, a few years later we had him as our parish priest until he went to Nelson in the interior of British Columbia and was made a bishop.

Getting to know you, getting to know all about you?

We had a small reception in our rented West End apartment with a dozen friends. I did self-catering courtesy of Woodward's department store. Friends cleared up the apartment, while David and I drove around Stanley Park. For our honeymoon we had planned to go to Europe in the spring and visit our parents, as neither of them had been able to attend the wedding.

The English and the German people have different habits in their daily lives and we had to get to know each other and adjust. The English drive on the left side of the road and walk on the left when crossing the street, whereas the Germans and the rest of Europeans drive on the right side of the street. Also, the English stand on the left side on escalators. As it happened, I learned to do what the English do. I still do it here in Canada and I am, therefore, a real nuisance when I am taking the escalator.

My great admiration goes to the English for lining up patiently at bus stops waiting for their turn to board. Not so in Germany! On a visit there, David was nearly left stranded without any money at a bus stop outside the Frankfurt main railway station, when a waiting crowd stormed the bus, pushing past my polite Englishman. Only my screams made the driver stop again and, fortunately, David got onto the bus. He would have been lost in my home town.

In May of 1961, we travelled to Europe to visit our respective parents-in-law, whom we had not yet met. We had driven through the States, left the car with relatives and taken an Italian liner to Venice. Almost everybody got seasick as soon as the ship left New York. The decks were closed because of the storm and the many returning Italians in their best suits were trapped underneath vomiting all over the place. It made poor David sick to see it and smell the mess. I managed to go outside to participate in a boat drill when a young woman with an English accent asked me: "Where is David?" I was surprised to learn that David knew somebody on the ship. She read my thoughts and added "We had met in Vancouver". When I learned later that she had transferred to a different class I asked myself how well they had known each other.

In Venice, at the end of the sea voyage, we stepped out into the world of our fore-fathers. At the pier there was a multitude of porters waiting to help the passengers to their respective destinations. We told our porter to find us a hotel in town. He nodded his head, heaved up one suitcase on his shoulder and with the other arm carried the heavy suitcases for some distance. It got very hot even though the sun had gone down. Just after crossing a small bridge, the porter stopped and nodded his head again. We paid a ridiculously small sum for his services. Our room was on the second floor. With a sigh I hit the bed and closed my eyes.

I was suddenly wide awake again. A tremendous noise came from downstairs: stamping of feet and singing at the same time! A party no doubt, I assumed. At midnight the party was over. I later learned that the bridge nearby is called "The Bridge of Sighs" by the locals. In his recently published bestselling book: *Inferno,* page 307, Dan Brown gives more insight: "The Bridge drew its name not from the sighs of passion, but from sighs of misery. As it turned out the enclosed walkway served as the connector between the Doge's Palace and the doge's prison, where the incarcerated languished and died, their groans of anguish echoed out of the grated windows along the narrow canal".

We spent a few days in Rome and toured the Vatican. The painted ceiling of the Sistine Chapel is fantastic. How could

Getting to know you, getting to know all about you?

Michelangelo have done it? The physical effort alone is daunting; standing or lying for hours on a scaffold, looking up, painting with an outstretched arm onto the ceiling his images of the creation of the world, and all the other different scenes from the Bible? On top of it, Pope Leo interfered and they had heated arguments. Recommended reading on the subject is the biographical historical novel *The Agony and the Ecstasy* by Irving Stone. I have in my apartment a print of Michelangelo's "Creation of the World" and I walk by it all the time. The huge custom-framed print gives me a lift from the routine of doing housework, but also reminds me how blessed I am to have met David. He is to my thinking my Prince, like the main character in the Grimms' Brothers' *Fairy Tales*. These stories were read to me in my childhood and many of the characters I keep meeting later in real life.

I must continue now to explore the world of Michelangelo to show you, dear Reader, my increased understanding of the arts. As I already mentioned in "My Journey to the New World", I only have only a grade 8 education due to the war years. After our three sons had graduated from university, I had more time of my own and I decided that it was my turn now. They only smiled and nodded their heads respectfully when I announced that I would follow in their foot-steps. Well, I enjoyed going to University and graduated in 1997 with a First Class Bachelor of Arts degree. The day of my graduation I still consider the second most wonderful day in my life. The first was getting married. Now I am beginning to wonder what my third most wonderful day might be. Yes, you guessed it, dear Reader, when my first book *My Journey to the New World* was published.

Thanks to my Fine Arts Course I know now that Michelangelo was not only a famous painter but also a remarkable sculptor. It was the "Pieta" which made his name as a sculptor. Chiselled from a block of marble, the dead figure of Christ spread out over the lap of his mother is horizontally balanced. The garment that is partly covering his nudity is pleated. The marble is beautifully polished. The artist had by 1500 already perfected the presentation of the human body. The "Pieta" made him a famous sculptor. I do not think that David enjoyed the religious art as much as I did; however, he never said so. On this later visit to the Vatican, we did not visit the Sistine Chapel because of a steep entrance fee, but I bought a beautiful crucifix from a sales stand outside which I treasure and wear a lot these days. I was told that it had been blessed by Pope John XXII.

We took the train to Frankfurt-am-Main, my hometown. My parents were delighted with their new son-in-law. There was, however, a language barrier. My mother spoke no English at all, whereas my father showed off the little he knew, like: "early to bed and early to rise makes the man happy, wealthy, and wise." Mother addressed David in a loud voice thinking he might therefore understand her better, but without success. While I had taught David some German on the long drive through the States by calling out and by him repeating the sights like *Autofriedhof* (car dump) and *Stadt* (town), his knowledge of the language was very limited. David was a good sport though. I knew in my heart he bathed in the love and affection my parents showed him. In retrospect, I am very proud of David's patience in his dealings with my Mum and Dad, who were quite different from his English parents back home, as I later learned.

I showed David around my home town. My former employer, British European Airways, had opened a large office in a somewhat obscure location. However, as it turned out later, the location became very visible when the street corner was incorporated in a new Plaza. To my surprise, my old colleague Miss Bachman was still working there, but was not on duty when

Getting to know you, getting to know all about you?

we came by. I don't think we dropped in at the British Centre. I felt a bit awkward to show myself – pregnant already! David was very interested in the rebuilt downtown area. Most of the car traffic through town went underground, as was the case with the parking. Frankfurt had arisen from the ashes and become a modern metropolis.

We flew into Gatwick airport south of London. A chauffeur-driven car took us to his parent's house in Chislehurst, just outside southeast London. When the driver stopped at the house, I looked out of the car window and told David I was not going in. I remember being scared. He smiled at me and said: "They will love you, dear." I said to myself: "I might as well go in. These beautiful roses have a caring gardener."

David's parents were sitting in the lounge, and, after entering, David's mother directed me to go upstairs to freshen up. As I was coming down, she looked very carefully at me and finally asked: "When is the baby due?" I did not think my pregnancy was showing yet. Clever woman, I thought. Well, I could set her mind at ease. Our first child was conceived after our marriage and was not due until November. I felt his mother would get to like me, as she seemed to be keen on having more grandchildren. On the other hand, she might have been curious: was this grandchild conceived before we had married? Had this unknown daughter-in-law from the Wild West thus made David marry her son? I must confess if I had been in her shoes I might have been suspicious like her.

I had noticed that David's mother was watching me again at the dining table. When she could no longer restrain herself, she said: "Gudy, here in England after we finish our meal we put our knife and fork together side by side on the plate", and she demonstrated it. In my ignorance of certain English customs, i.e.

table manners, I had left my fork and knife resting on the plate with the handles of each on the tablecloth. I bit my tongue and only said "Thank you, Mother." David had never corrected me and I now felt nervous. To calm myself I went into the vegetable garden in the back to inspect it, pulled out the odd weed and looked in awe at the fast ripening tomatoes. They reminded me of the growing baby inside me and I relaxed. It was really not a big issue if she did not like my table manners. I was going back to Canada.

David's father said we could use the "company" car during our stay with them. The small car proved to be very handy. However, the first time we drove it down the local road, I saw in the rear window that David's mother was running after us and frantically pointing to the other side of the road. David stopped and, when she reached us, she was out of breath and gasped: "David, in this country we drive on the left". This time it was David's turn to say: "Thank you, Mother. I am sorry".

To get David accustomed to driving on the left side of the road we decided to go to Canterbury Cathedral on the byways and avoid the fast roads. This particular byway was called Pilgrims Way. The road was narrow and whenever we saw a vehicle going the other way, David would pull over to let the other car go by. As we were slowly driving along the lane, I was suddenly reminded of *The Canterbury Tales* written by Geoffrey Chaucer as long ago as 1386.

The Introduction to *The Canterbury Tales* given in the Norton Anthology of English Literature, fourth edition, Volume I, describes forty-nine pilgrims on horseback riding through the countryside one evening in April. They are on their way from London to the big cathedral in Canterbury, where Archbishop Thomas Becket was murdered in 1170 by four knights of King

Getting to know you, getting to know all about you?

Henry II. The furious King had cried out: "Will no one rid me of this troublesome priest," and the knights obliged.

In Chaucer's story some of the pilgrims tell tales to pass the time as they made their way to the Cathedral. I found the tale of the Wife of Bath very enlightening. Like Mother Courage of the later Thirty Years War, (1618 – 1648), the Wife of Bath was a feminist. She demanded that the wife should be in command of her husband and that the husband should be obedient to her. This statement offended the male pilgrims and the subject was discussed further in more detail. The debate finally ended when both sides agreed that "tolerance" should be practiced by both husband and wife. I conclude that the Middle Ages were not as dark as the historians might want us to believe.

When the pilgrims arrived at their destination they probably headed right away to the crypt containing the shrine of the slain Archbishop Becket. David and I did not get so far! On entering the huge Cathedral we were stopped again in our track by the height of the massive church. The Cathedral is partly Romanesque and partly Gothic. The official name is Metro Political Church of Christ at Canterbury. After a quick walk around the interior, we were lured outside by the sunlight shining in. Monastic buildings were incorporated into the church building. A cloister is actually attached to the cathedral and has a stone walkway surrounding one side of the cathedral. We were very impressed. As it was getting late and we had not had lunch yet, David proposed we come back another day.

As it turned out, David and I visited Canterbury Cathedral many times in later years. The Cathedral was near to Chislehurst and the Old Peoples Home in which his mother stayed for ten years after she had broken both hips. On one of our visits, David said: "Do you still play bridge, Mother?" A shadow passed over her face and she replied: "No, they are all so old here". In fact, she was the oldest and had long been the longest patient there.

I had better return to literature again. Both Geoffrey Chaucer and another great man of English literature, William Shakespeare, were busy men of the world. How did they find time to write so many plays, and poems that have withstood the changes in public tastes? The identity of the medieval poet Geoffrey Chaucer has been firmly established, However, Shakespeare remains a mystery person. We have portraits of him, but not much more. Yet he is the greatest English poet. It is impossible to look at any one of his plays or poetry in detail within the scope of this Journal.

I came across one poem that is short enough and reminded me at the same time of the German poet and writer Johann Wolfgang von Goethe. He was a contemporary of Shakespeare. It is like most of Goethe's works, in the romantic mood:

> "Where the bee sucks, there suck I:
> In a cowslip's bell I lie;
> There I crouch when owls do cry.
> On the bat's back do I fly
> After summer merrily.
> Merrily, merrily shall I live now
> Under the blossom that hangs on the bough".

So much has been written lately in our daily papers about Shakespeare as a poet, but also to my great surprise, as an unpleasant businessman. On April 11, 2013, the *Financial Post* newspaper published an article by Antoni Cimolimo, the artistic director of the Stratford Festival headed "A Portrait of the Artist as a Tax Dodger". Shakespeare's work may be sublime, but when it came down to the world of business, he knew how to make a

Getting to know you, getting to know all about you?

fast buck. Ha, ha, they found him out after all, I said aloud. He took so much care to cover up his identity, but it may be in vain in the end. Antoni Cimolimo only echoes the London *Sunday Telegraph* which came out with the headline "Bad Bard: a tax dodger and profiteer". The Sunday Telegraph informed its readers that in the old days the English theatre people were described in legislation as "rogues, vagabonds, and sturdy beggars". Nevertheless, you cannot take away the fact that he was "a brilliant dramatist: a careful observer of human nature, a man of extraordinary wit, talent and originality." Tax scandals then and now are very interesting indeed!

Sometimes during a conversation when I talk with friends or even strangers about world events I have developed the habit of brushing events off with Shakespeare's own clever observation:

> "All the world's a stage
> And all the men and women merely players:
> They have their exists and their entrances;
> And one man in his time plays many parts".

Of all the plays by Shakespeare I like best the tragedy of *Romeo and Juliet* as a ballet. In the April 2013 edition of *Readers Digest*, a story recounts that tourists, especially young girls, are flocking to the town of Verona in Italy. They head for the house where Juliet lived and stare up to the balcony where from below Romeo told her of his love for her. Dear Reader, I have not met any characters before in an English poet's literary work who reminded me of the Grimm's *Fairy Tales*. We actually attended in London a performance of the ballet in 2003 and this is what the program had to say:

"Shakespeare's tragedy of the star-crossed lovers has inspired generations of leading artists from Gounod to Peggy Ashcroft to

Baz Luhrmann; Kenneth McMillan is no exception. Marrying the play and Prokofiev's passionate, brooding score, he produced a classic of 20th-century choreography and one of the Royal Company's most popular works, all more remarkable considering it was his first full-length ballet. *Pas de deux* of startling lyrical beauty are danced against a spectacular and forceful portrait of Renaissance Italy and a city torn apart by factionalism. Romeo, a member of the aristocratic Montague family, impulsively gate-crashes a ball given by his family's enemies, the Capulet's, only to fall in love with their daughter, the wilful Juliet. The lovers are secretly married but any hopes that their union might lead to harmony are shattered when Juliet's vicious cousin Tybalt kills Mercutio fighting for Romeo's cause. The lovers' attempts to escape from the ensuing violence lead to tragedy."

Having been an aspiring ballet dancer myself, as I mentioned in my earlier book, I realized I could never have been a professional dancer. I am neither light in weight, nor am I small. Another girl in our ballet class, who was light but not small, had long legs. She did become a professional dancer though always in the chorus line. I knew her fairly well and when we met again, she had become a fitness instructor, i.e. she retired from ballet early.

Why do I find that the main characters in Romeo and Juliet by Shakespeare compare to "Rapunzel" in the folktale by the Brothers Grimm? They all were lovers with people opposed to their union. Romeo and Juliet did get married but did not "live happily ever after". The king's son had heard Rapunzel sing while passing by and wanted to see her. Rapunzel let her long hair out of the window and he climbed up (Print enclosed). *Grimm's Fairy Tales*, from the 1883 translation from the German by Lucy Crane, illustrated by Scott McKowen. He fell in love with the untouched maiden and ended up visiting her every evening in the high tower. One day, as her wicked stepmother visited her to bring

Getting to know you, getting to know all about you?

food, Rapunzel said out loud what she only should have asked herself quietly: why are my clothes getting too tight? All came to light! Her hair was cut off. Her lover tried to jump up but fell to

the ground into a thorn hedge. His eyes were pierced by thorns and he no longer could see, nor could he find his way home. Rapunzel bore a daughter and a son. One day when she was outside she recognized his voice in the distance. On finding him, she saw his misfortune, took him in her arms and sat down. Rapunzel started to cry. Tears touched his eyes and he began to see again. The prince returned home to the king with Rapunzel and the children: "they lived happily ever after" but they had experienced great sorrow before they were granted eternal bliss!

One explanation for why stepmothers were treating their daughters so badly was the high mortality rate of mothers when giving birth in the old days. When the men re-married and had children with their second wife, all attention was given to this off-spring, while the others are ignored or mistreated.

I was still trying to find English replacements for the folk tales of the Brothers Grimm. *Alice in Wonderland* written by Lewis Carroll was my first choice. The heroine is watching a white rabbit hurrying by as she and her sister are resting on a meadow. While watching the rabbit run back and forth, like her sister,

Gudrun Honig

Alice falls asleep. In her dreams she follows the rabbit down a rabbit hole. She shrinks in size and down, down, down, she falls deep through the ground. During the following adventures down below, she had to change her height. (Everyman's Library, Alfred Knope, New York, London, Toronto, 1992. Illustrations are by John Tennil).

As I could not warm up to the character of Alice, I sadly dropped her from my list. I greatly enjoyed the illustrations in the book I was reading, however, in the cruise ship's library showing Alice shrinking, growing very tall, and finally, shrinking again in order to go back above ground. Tolkien's *Hobbit* has just been filmed and is a box-office hit. The story also takes place underground. For my purposes it is not an ideal place to be. Therefore, I dropped the popular tale as well.

I must stop here! I have gone astray again, off the right path just like Red Riding Hood. The result was she is nearly eaten by that beast, who in my first book was Adolf Hitler, the leader of the wolf pack, the storm troopers, who sniffed out the Jews and took control of the German Reich.

I decided to take the advice of my instructor Alison Acheson and my co-participant Nikita in my excellent Journal Writing course at Capilano University in North Vancouver, B.C. to stay with my archetypes, i.e. primordial images shaped in myths, religions and dreams which I found in the Grimm Brothers' *Folk Fairy Tales*.

Getting to know you, getting to know all about you?

Like most German children of the last century, I knew these tales almost by heart. All started with "Once upon a time and ended" with "they lived happily ever after". Hitler supported the tales because in his opinion they reflected nationalistic ideas: obedience, discipline, authoritarian, militarism, and glorification of violence (*The New Yorker*, July 23, 2012).

I am back again in London. The next day I said I would like to go "up" to London to see Buckingham Palace. We travelled by train and at the terminus I noticed a big column nearby. David told me that it was Nelson's Column and was outside the National Gallery. I recalled immediately the beautiful fresco by Michelangelo in the Sistine Chapel and desired to see more of the same. However, we passed by the medieval religious paintings, because they looked static by comparison with Michelangelo's religious paintings.

Suddenly, I stopped in my tracks: I had spotted a locomotive engulfed in steam, hardly visible in the rain, coming towards me. It was entitled: "Rain, Steam and Speed - The Great Western Railway" by J.M.W. Turner. He is a late romantic, pre-impressionist landscape painter. To show the viewer a speedy train going along hardly visible under its steam and the rain, Turner succeeded. However, this image unfortunately does not give the painter credit in his treatment of colour on canvas, which makes him a pre-impressionist. I was lucky enough to see more of his art on later occasions in the London Tate Gallery. Incidentally, Turner died a rich man, unlike most painters, who die poor. The value of their paintings, however, skyrocketed after their death. Turner died in the house of his mistress and is buried in St. Paul's Cathedral.

David's father suggested we go up to London again on the Queen's official birthday of June 24th. Since we had a few days in hand before that date, we took walks around Chislehurst. It is located in a park-like setting, next to a "common". We never met any walkers in this set-aside large area of land. One can find parks designated as commons in other places in England. On one of these early morning rounds we spotted a small monument. William Willett, the inventor of Daylight Saving Time lived nearby. Sir Winston Churchill, the great statesman, saluted him because, with the introduction of daylight saving time, longer working hours were possible in the production of essential war materials. By advancing the clocks one hour in the spring and retarding them one hour in the fall one hundred and fifty four daylight working hours were gained each year. The Observatory in Greenwich is a great place to visit to find out more about daylight saving time and clocks.

Hadrian's Wall is arguably the most important and best preserved monument in England. The Wall was built by the order of the Emperor Hadrian in AD 122. It is 117 km long. It was built to prevent the people from the north entering England and is really the northern boundary of the Roman Empire. By about AD 400 the Holy Roman Empire began to crumble. Settlement patterns changed. Building stones from Hadrian's Wall can be found in houses and churches. The Wall was designated a World Heritage site in 1987.

As I wrote in my previous book, on a skiing trip into the Taunus, my father had showed me on our local mountains by my hometown of Frankfurt, the remains of the Roman Wall sticking out from under the snow. Unfortunately, I cannot recall whether he took us to the *Saalburg* as promised. I doubt very much the Roman fortification in the Taunus were on a scale like Hadrian's fortifications. The reconstructed ruins were probably that of a garrison.

Getting to know you, getting to know all about you?

It seems that in Great Britain there is so much history to be discovered, much more than in Germany. Elizabeth Alexandra Mary, Queen of the United Kingdom of Great Britain and Northern Ireland and of her other Realms and Territories, Head of the Commonwealth, shows us the vast domain over which the Queen reigns. In Germany the top boss was simply named Kaiser Wilhelm Friedrich, King of Prussia. I read somewhere that Prussia, i.e. Germany, was the last big power to get its grip on colonies. My social housing estate of Westhausen had its streets named after our colonies: *Neu Guinea Weg, Togo Weg* and *Samoa Weg* are the ones I remember. After World War II these streets were re-named; *Geschwister Scholl Strasse, Kaethe Colwitz* and other persons who died in German concentration camps. By the way, not only Jews but also students were opposed to Fascism, like the above named *Geschwister Scholl.*

Hetty, David oldest aunt, wanted to meet me. Her small house was just outside Richmond Park in Kingston and very close to the river Thames. We went by car and David had lost his way there, so we arrived a little bit late. When we entered the garden, I saw a huge bird cage at the back of her house. It was crowded with canaries of different varieties. The gardener/chauffeur let us in. He actually looked like a big dwarf; on his nose was a huge cancerous growth. Hetty, too, was small in stature. Both the gardener and David's aunt could have stepped out of the Grimms Fairy Tales. Next to the dining room table stood an antique stand laden with delicately made sandwiches - smoked salmon! David tucked in and so did I. Amazingly, we could even eat some of the cakes. No, I did not feel guilty, as I was eating for two!

The conversation was pleasant until Hetty jumped up and said: "I must turn on the television. Sybil's horse is running and I have a bet on her". How exciting it was to watch the Derby, not only the running horses but also the beautiful people and their hats! Now

Gudrun Honig

I truly cannot remember whether Sybil's horse won or lost. If the mare lost, what could five pounds matter to Hetty? If the horse won, she was just an excuse to phone and to congratulate her youngest sister. Anyway, we had to get going to avoid the rush hour traffic. The gardener saw us out and opened the car door for me (photo; Hetty, Sybil and Elsie). David told me that neither Hetty nor Sybil got married. Hetty helped to looked after the younger children and Sybil took care after mother later on. Since we had not heard when it would be convenient for us to visit Sybil or Elsie. We had time to see David's boarding school, Berkhamsted, northwest of London.

David and his brother Michael were boarders at the college from age 13 until they were required to enlist in the army at age 18. At school Michael was often one grade higher than David, because Michael was born in January and David in December of the same year. They went home by train to Bromley on the southeast edge of London for school holidays and for half-term holidays. Crossing London meant using a train to get to London, travelling by Tube (underground trains) across London, and going by another train to Bromley. David and Michael travelled

Getting to know you, getting to know all about you?

together with Michael leading. When Michael went into the army a year before David, David did not know which trains to catch; he had to learn fast, because he was on his own from then on.

Again the company car proved very useful on our visit. There were no boys running about, but the Assembly Hall was unlocked. As I looked up, I was frightened by pairs of male eyes in great numbers looking down at me. David explained to me that all these portraits were of former headmasters of the college. Suddenly, I saw her! The current head was a woman. Was David surprised? I am not sure. I began to realize that my husband is difficult to read!

Soon after the Second World War started, Dulwich College Preparatory School, which was the school David and Michael attended until they reached the age of 13, was evacuated to Betws-y-Coed, in North Wales. About the same time I was also evacuated in Germany for the same reason: to get away to a safe place. On another visit to England, David took me to North Wales to show me Betws-y-Coed, which is actually a tourist spot and very scenic. Because Dulwich is southeast of London and in line with German

airplanes flying to drop bombs on London, the headmaster took over The Royal Oak Hotel, the best hotel in Betws-y-Coed (print). The boys had to provide their own beds, which were folding ones to enable the beds to be transported by train. From time to time these beds would collapse in the night, the collapse usually caused by other boys' mischievousness. The boys slept in the hotel and the classes were held in rooms over the stables. There were no playing fields, but the ingenious teachers were able to think up various outdoor activities. The adventure did no harm to the boys' education and was obviously enjoyed by them, because the now-elderly ex-school boys still meet there every year. On a postcard of Betws-y-Coed the place is described as a Fairy Tale village.

In a new book about the British Empire, Kwasi Kwarteng mentions how important it is for one's career to be able to speak the King's English (Ghosts of Empire: Britain's Legacies in the Modern World). The author George Orwell puts it even more dramatically, writing: "Unless you went to a good public school, you were ruined for life." (In England a public school is a private school!) For these reasons English parents pay high fees to get their children into private schools. I met somebody in Bromley who had six children. Bromley is the nearest market town to Chislehurst. When I asked her if she had any help in the house, she said she didn't. She saw my surprise and explained that she did not want her children to hear poor English spoken, as they might copy the accent of her helper. I could understand her reasoning, because I had accompanied David on a visit to the home of his parent's retired house-help, Mrs Cowlard.

Mrs Cowlard and David carried on a lively conversation about the good old days; the chain-smoking lady had been with the family for twenty-five years and when she retired, was given a golden watch, which I duly admired. After we left, David asked me

Getting to know you, getting to know all about you?

whether I had enjoyed the visit. He was surprised when I told him that I had not understood a word that the former employee had said, because of her accent. It was to David's credit that he visited the family's former household employee and showed his appreciation for her loyal service to the family.

David's parents played tennis at Bromley Cricket Club, which had grounds for both cricket and tennis. Fred and Muriel were very good tennis players and won many tournaments and several trophies, i.e. cups. By the time we visited them they had switched from tennis to golf. I saw his mother practicing her golf strokes in the back of the garden. I had learned by then that golf is serious business to most players and not just fun. David and I tried this popular sport when we lived in England in the early seventies. I was not without skill to play golf, but frankly, I found it very boring. David did not take to it either. I am happy to say he does not go off, like so many retired men, to play golf all day while their wives play bridge.

The clubhouse of Chislehurst Golf Club at Camden Place, very near to David's parent's home, has a very interesting history. I actually could not believe my ears when I was told that Napoleon III, nephew of Napoleon Bonaparte, lived and died in the mansion, which became the clubhouse. He was captured by the Prussians in 1870 after losing at the Battle of Sedan and was deposed as Emperor. For six months he was held prisoner and then spent his last few years in exile at Camden Place.

As I mentioned, after we had been to David and Michael's college, we then continued our trip to the picturesque Lake District, where we came upon an extraordinary sight: a beautifully placed ring of twenty-eight massive rocks on a plateau outside Keswick. The "Breaker" folk in megalithic times were thought to have built this impressive stone circle in about 1500 BC.

Getting to know you, getting to know all about you?

We went on to Scotland where, in one town, a parade was in progress. Scots in their colourful uniforms were playing their bagpipes and drums, cheered on by many onlookers.

I use here some information provided by the tourist office about the ancient culture of the Scots, who are descended from the

Gudrun Honig

"Picts", who inhabited Scotland at the time the Romans conquered England. Since 1707, Scotland has been part of the United Kingdom. Although governed from London, Scotland has, however, retained many of its own laws, its own educational system and its own Christian church: Presbyterian. The population of Scotland today is about five million. However, because of lack of opportunities, over the centuries many emigrated and, about twenty million are spread around the world. Robert Burns, Scotland's national poet, tells of the sentiments Scots have for their homeland:

> "My heart is in the Highlands.
> My heart is not here;
> My heart's in the Highlands
> A-chasing the deer;
> Chasing the wild deer,
> And following the roe
> My heart is in the Highlands,
> Wherever I go."

Quite obviously, Burns describes the homesickness of the Scots who left the highlands. I had to look it up to do some hard thinking. Here is my interpretation: A revolution in the sheep-based agricultural practices resulted in clearances of land and the tenants had to leave, often in a hurry. These clearances were carried out by hereditary aristocratic landowners. The changes were seen to be supported by the government, which gave financial aid for roads and bridges to assist the new agriculture based on sheep and trade. As I mentioned in my family history in my earlier book, my mother's village in Germany was also taken over by higher authorities. Adolf Hitler, who expanded the military base of Hammelburg, compensated everybody for the land and homes they were forced to give up. It looks to me that dictatorship had dealt more fairly with the clearance of land. I

Getting to know you, getting to know all about you?

am surprised that the Scots are yearning for the Highlands after they received such bad treatment from the landowners and the British government.

I remember that we ended up in Edinburgh on this particular trip. We stayed on the campus with some soccer teams and had a delicious buffet breakfast; it was the first time I had smoked herring ("kippers") for breakfast. We also toured Edinburgh Castle, which Prince Albert had rebuilt for his wife, Queen Victoria. On our free tour of the town we made friends with a local couple who invited us back to their home for a drink. He was a retired sea captain and writing a book, I believe. His wife, like me, attended university classes working towards a degree.

We flew home via Frankfurt and, strolling about the *Altstadt* (old town), we noticed a large crowd assembled outside the rebuilt *Roemer* where Charles the Great had crowned himself Holy Roman Emperor in the year 800. When I asked a bystander in German what was happening, he gave me no answer. Only when I told him we were from abroad did he explain in a jubilant voice: "Our local soccer team, the *Eintracht*, won the European Soccer Championship". I even found a newspaper cutting showing the Queen congratulating the team in London and handing its captain the trophy. Another article tells us of the English people rioting in London in the streets. Isn't the Queen a good sport? While the English and the Germans share the excitement of the "beautiful game," only the English people have a Queen. We have just watched on television a re-run of her coronation sixty years ago; she was so young when she ascended the throne. "Our Gracious Queen" has seen so many changes in the world at large and at home. I do admire her dignity and humour. David told me that I was a Royalist. Ha, I am also impressed – a woman on the throne of Britain and now also the Head of the Anglican Church! Can you imagine anything more exciting?

Gudrun Honig

What is wrong about being a Royalist? I insisted we visit Windsor Castle, the official residence of the Queen. We travelled by train from Paddington Station in London. The Queen guards her privacy not only behind a high wall but also by the high admission fee. No, there was no reduction as compensation for the closed Chapel due to restoration. The flag was up and blowing in the wind. The guide confirmed that she was in residence and he had seen her in the morning playing with her dogs on the lawn. As a matter of fact, he continued, she is just beyond this wall here. The huge antique dolls house looked as it had never been played with. The short tour had ended and the small number of tourist left through a side door. Well, I could now say: "I have been there".

David told me that on many Saturdays he would go with his father to watch a soccer match when Michael was in the army. The beautiful game does many wonderful things. Now our grandson Harrison is a very good soccer player; he has an athletic scholarship and attends the University of British Columbia, Kelowna Campus. His father, our son Peter, is a certified referee, but none of my other grandsons has taken it up seriously yet (photo).We just had such an exciting phone call from our son Peter. He was informed by the British Columbia Soccer Association that he has been chosen to receive the annual Award of Merit for 2012/2013. It will be presented to him during the next Vancouver Whitecaps match at B.C. Place. The e-mail continues to state that these awards are presented to individuals in recognitions of contributions to soccer, during a period of ten or more years, as a player, manager, coach, official or administrator at the club, league or district level.

Our dear Peter asked us: "Why me?" I said that the committee knew what it was doing! Peter actually started out as a Cricket

Getting to know you, getting to know all about you?

and Rugby player when he attended school in England, but the beautiful game became his choice in sports. He was allowed to bring one guest to presentation of the award and he asked his Dad. It is also a reward for parents to see their children do well professionally and socially in their community.

Our family has considered flying to the Old Country this summer to see the Land of their Fathers, so to speak. I keep hearing in the night: "Here is the BBC. This is London calling", but we have to be realistic! After all I have all these beautiful photographs of our former visits. As I write about these trips my memories are coming back, for that is why I keep on taking photos. I might start a series of travel books, like "Travels with Gudrun" showing all the places we have been to. I am afraid I shall be forced to be an armchair traveller from now on, which is a lot safer these days.

A tourist needs only to stay in London, where history is spread out before you right along on the banks of the Thames. Other historic places are within easy reach by public transport and certainly preferable to using a car. Remember, in England you will have to drive on the left and it is easily forgotten once you turn off the main roads to travel the by-ways. Also, when you are on foot and crossing the street, first look left, then right, then left again, otherwise you may be run over.

My point is that there is so much to see in the capital of Britain alone that one single holiday is not enough to take it all in. Luckily, there is free information available from the tourist office to help strangers find their way and explore what London has to offer. David and I were very thankful for the hand-outs by the Tourist Office as we explored the Southbank of the river Thames.

Gudrun Honig

The Tate Modern Gallery, once a power station, contains six hundred works of art. The transformation of nearby Southwark and its Riverside walk with its various exhibits is for the visitor on  English history lesson and a pleasure ground for the locals. While new pubs and bars have replaced the former inns, the remains of old buildings like the Clink Prison are still there. An exhibit reminds the curious of the privateers, like Sir Walter Raleigh (1554-1680) a favourite of Queen Elizabeth I. A full-scale replica of his sailing ship "The Golden Hinde" is now moored further along at St. Mary Overlie (photo). London Bridge is a legend by its very name, but it did not fall down in spite of what this nursery rhyme says: "London Bridge is falling down falling down, falling down my fair lady".

The Bridge was torn down to make way for a new structure probably more than once. Developers in the American town Lake Havasu City maintain that their place is the most successful new town in the United States. The new town of only twenty-five thousand needed a tourist attraction. They bought the London Bridge in 1967 for $2,460,000, disassembled it, then transported it to Lake Havasu City and reassembled it. Finally, they dredged a canal so that water could flow underneath it. This folly became a success and we even made a detour to see it.

Getting to know you, getting to know all about you?

Continuing up the Thames one passes the rebuilt open-air Shakespeare Theatre and the Festival Hall. Let us, however, continue for now because we have spotted the latest attraction ahead of us: the London Eye. The capsules are aero-dynamically enclosed, my old newspaper article explains. It was a clear day when brave David rode it. He told me the twelve capsules take twenty six passengers each. He raved about the view. He also said that he was sorry that I had not come with him! It made me very happy. We chose to eat at McDonalds, as it was right there, next to the London Eye and went back to see the Festival Centre. This new modern building is another jewel on the historical Southbank's walk: in the round, spacious, airy, wardrobes, refreshments and live musical entertainment while you wait for your performance to start.

We have seen a number of good plays there like "Vincent in Brixton". (Vincent Van Gogh was the Dutch painter. If I remember rightly, he had an affair with the landlady. No, dear Reader, the landlady was not French and not young. Yes, she was over-the-hill and English!) Oh, oh, while I am talking about such a topical subject, namely SEX, this might be a good place to relate what I saw when we lived in a rented house in an upper-middle-class area near London in the early seventies before Mrs. Thatcher came to power (her state funeral was yesterday, Saturday, the 20th of April, 2013)!

Getting to know you, getting to know all about you?

The home owners next door were a middle-aged couple and, like most English people, proud of their garden. One sunny day I looked out of the upper window, when I saw the owner standing on a low ladder and handing down the beautiful summer apples one by one to his wife who put them all, one by one in a basket. A scene of domestic bliss! At midnight I was woken up by the calls of help from a female voice. I rushed to the front door not realizing that the calls of help had come from the garden next door. By the time I made it to our front door, the calls of help came from down the road. However, I was just in time to see our athletic neighbour run down the road in hot pursuit a figure wearing a long white robe. Realizing there was nothing I should do, I went back to bed. Another neighbour across the street said to me the next day: "After what happened last night, I am afraid we will not be able to sell our house when this story gets out".

The last time we were in London, we saw what is to date my favourite play: "England People Very Nice". The following notes are from the program. "The play is a journey through time. Four waves of immigration as early as the 17th century come to England. As the French Huguenots, the Irish, the Jews, and the Bangladeshis come to the world of Bethnal Green in East London each new influx provokes a surge of protest over housing, religion, and culture." The English audience just laughed off the criticism hurled at them by the actors on the stage. In reality, the immigrants brought new skills and established themselves more or less successfully sooner or later. Some brought new culinary skills. Locals and the English developed a taste for different food and started to shy away from the traditional greasy fish and chips wrapped in newspaper.

David's parents took us out to eat several times at "The Bull," a local pub. He told me the way to identify a good restaurant is by the hot plates when your order arrives. To this day I follow his advice. I was surprised when a small trolley was brought in on which lay the most delicious desserts, unknown to me, like boiled pears, various tarts, etc., all for us to choose from. I wonder now, how David put up with my ice cream and fresh fruit. He is so patient and tolerant.

Ha, ha, *Eureka*, I have got it! The key to happiness in a marriage is TOLERANCE; personally, I like to add two other factors: namely, to have CHILDREN and GRANDCHILDREN. The latter, are a reward for having had children in the first place. Amen.

TOLERANCE was also agreed upon by the Pilgrims on their way to Canterbury as early as 1386 as a prerequisite to a successful marriage. Do you remember the arguments, dear Friends? I don't know why all of a sudden the magic word came from, but TOLERANCE it is!

Let us go back to our walk along the river Thames. We had by-passed the newly built Shakespeare Theatre because we had seen the London Eye ahead of us and hurried there first. The theatre was built in the original style. Nevertheless, it looked phony to me. I did not like the idea of walking about during a play. I do not know whether we actually attended a

Getting to know you, getting to know all about you?

performance. We were not missed, as the performances were very popular.

Another attraction not to be missed is the British Museum; it is somewhat off the beaten track, but buses go there. Again the museum advertises itself: "Museum-visiting was never like this! The Museum's glass- and steel-roofed Great Court brings ultra-modern pizzazz to its venerable collections. How about a champagne or tea while you are here"?

ABOVE LEFT Museum-visiting was never like this! The British Museum's glass-and-steel-roofed Great Court brings ultra-modern pizzazz to its venerable collections. How about a champagne tea while you're here?

Gudrun Honig

Yes, we had tea and rested our feet. Ever since the Elgin Marbles collection had been put together by Lord Elgin in 1806 the controversy has been going on to this very day! After the collection arrived in Britain some critics accused the collector of vandalism, while others supported him. The British Parliament in the end decided that the Greek treasures should go to the British Museum (photo). Here they have remained for public viewing since 1816. We did not realize at the time when we saw these antiquities in the Museum that we would visit Greece one day and see the sites were they came from. Thus is life; full of surprises.

FROM ANCIENT EGYPT
The Rosetta Stone, the first key to reading hieroglyphs; giant sculptures of the pharaohs, paintings and mummies from the tombs.

The Rosetta stone, another valuable exhibit, is placed right next to the entrance door to the British Museum. In 1799 soldiers of Napoleon's army found the stone when digging for new fortifications in Egypt. After Napoleon's defeat the Stone became the property of the British Army under the Treaty of Alexandria two years later. The French scholar Francois Champollion realized that the other languages cut into the Stone in 196 BC were clues to deciphering the Egyptian hieroglyphs, which are figures of objects representing a word or sound or syllables. Credit goes to Champollion for deciphering the hieroglyphs on the Rosetta

Getting to know you, getting to know all about you?

stone, because it enabled us to explore the past: the story of the Egyptian culture.

Germany has its great Museum in its capital as well. We have been in Berlin before and after the Wall came down. It is on the Museum Island and dates back to the same period as the British Museum. The monumental Museum, however, lacked enough artefacts to fill the spacious halls. According to C.M. Ceram, author of Gods, Graves and Scholars, it began like a fairy tale! "The poor boy, who at the age of seven dreamed of finding a city, and thirty-nine years later went forth, sought, and found not only a city but also treasure such as the world had not seen since the loot of the *Conquistadors*."

The fairy tale is the story of Heinrich Schliemann, one of the most astounding personalities, not only among archaeologists, but among all men to whom any science has ever been indebted. Schliemann's exciting discoveries of Troy, of Olympia and Pergamum (Bergama), in Turkey and the exciting discovery of treasures in Babylon by Robert Koldewey gave the Germans enough antique pieces to fill the museums on *Insel*

Gudrun Honig

Island in Berlin. I now remember the blue *Ishtardoes* Gate of Babylon that towered over us as we entered the Pergamum Museum, when we were on a one day pass to East Berlin. We also saw the play/musical "Cabaret", written by Kurt Weil at the *Kurfuersterndam*; it had just started and we got in. We sometimes have incredible luck.

Let us continue with our exploration of London. By the year 2000, London had a new bridge. The narrow span was only for pedestrians. The new Millennium Bridge is the first new crossing in central London since the inauguration of the Tower Bridge in 1894. That is the one with the gothic towers each end and I often called London Bridge, which in the old days had shops in the middle of the span. If you cross it you can easily reach St. Paul's Cathedral.

David always proved a good guide. He had worked in London and, therefore, knew it well. In contrast, his younger brother, Peter, does not know London at all, because he had always worked in Bromley. I was very lucky indeed to have such an

Getting to know you, getting to know all about you?

informed husband as a guide. He loved to show me his town, just as my Dad had loved to show me my hometown: Frankfurt am Main.

St. Paul's Cathedral in the City of London was burned down by the Great Fire of London in 1666 and it took 35 years to re-build. Christopher Wren was the architect and it turned out to be a spectacular building, rising up 360 ft, second only in size amongst cathedrals in the world to St. Peter's in Rome. St. Paul's dominates the north side of the river, especially at summer evenings when it is floodlit. We only dropped in, but did not take the tour because of the fee. Here is a valuable tip for you, dear friend, go into a cathedral whenever there is a service and you see the inside without paying, unless of course you are well off and like to contribute to the maintenance of these ancient buildings. We did it many times and were able to attend Westminster Cathedral adjacent to the Parliament buildings more than once. It is a wonderful experience to attend in the service and above all, you can rest your feet!

Another option as a tourist is to take a river cruise: "A Voyage through History" says the advertisement. The view of the Millennium Dome and Thames Flood Barrier were our choice. The Millennium Dome is an entertainment complex seating 20,000 people and was used every day during the 2012 Summer Olympics. The Thames Flood Barrier is London's principal defence against the increasingly high tides coming up the Thames (photo). We once took a river cruise with our children and could not get back to the city by boat; the water was too high and the riverboat could not pass under the brides. The Flood Barrier became operational in November 1982. Twelve weeks later it had to be engaged to safeguard the city from a high tide which would have flooded the shorelines and buildings next to the river.

Gudrun Honig

The riverboat passes Hampton Court Palace on the way to the Thames Flood Barrier. Royal boats used to start from this royal palace and float down to the City of Westminster. This event was a favourite pastime for the Royal family and their entourage at the time and, no doubt, spectacular to watch on a summer evening. "For over five hundred years the palace has stood by the river banks there. Many important historical figures have fallen helplessly for their charms. Will you join them?" says another advertisement. We could not resist and did go in! However, I was disappointed. The long endless corridors in the palace were tiring and there was very little to see in the way of furniture or other antiques. However, when we went out of the back of the Palace I was very impressed by the sixty acres of Palace gardens: there was a Maze – it took us a long time to find our way out again between the trimmed high hedges – a great vine and of course, a garden shop. I nearly forgot to mention the tea shop which was a welcome sight.

Dear Reader, let us go back to our honeymoon trip. On the 24th of June we did go up to London to watch the Queen's official birthday celebration. It was quite a long walk and a hot day. I found walking no longer easy because of my pregnancy and the parade had started when we got to Buckingham Palace. However, I was able to take a photo of the Queen over the heads of the spectators as she was on horseback and visible above the heads of the crowd.

Getting to know you, getting to know all about you?

I was exhausted by the time we got back to Chislehurst. David is a fast walker and, just like my Dad, finds it difficult to slow down.

I decided it was time to go back to the New World as we had the long drive across the continent ahead of us: New York to Vancouver. Yet we had one more visit to make: to David's aunt, Elsie, who lived in Sidmouth, Devon, in southwest England. On the way there we stopped at an old church in the village of Easton in southern England. David's father had told us that his family came from Easton. With a chuckle he added that he had looked into his family genealogy, but had discontinued when he found out that the earliest Shrimpton on the list had been hanged; he had been a highwayman.

The well-known poet, R.B.H. Fuller, who assisted and succeeded David's father as the solicitor for the Woolwich Equitable Building Society, wrote his predecessor's obituary.

"Fred Shrimpton, who died on August 9, 1985, was the last of the senior executives who engineered the remarkable expansion in the late twenties and throughout the thirties, so with him an epoch ends.

"I am sure that Harold Kembel, whom he trained to be his valued personal assistant, would agree with me in thinking him the soundest lawyer ever encountered.

"He was in the Army on active service in the First World War (and served part-time in the Observer Corps in the Second) and afterwards was articled in the great law firm of Withers and Co.

"In appearance he was of almost unchanging youthfulness and neatness. He had been a very fine tennis player; was just turning over to golf when I first knew him, and came to love this game to. He disliked very much anything that smacked of pretentiousness or boastfulness. He gained respect by simply being himself. His staff (whose long service is legendary) held him in profound affection.

"He was lucky in (and proud of) his wife Muriel, and his three sons, who survive him and to whom our sympathy goes. One says "lucky", but here again Fred's discriminating choice, and patience in passing on his qualities, may be said to have operated as usual."

Getting to know you, getting to know all about you?

On his retirement from the Woolwich Building Society the employees gave David's father an engraved silver salver.

David's father was also a great help to Muriel, his wife, in the kitchen. He would put on an apron and help her wash-up the dishes after lunch. I can still see them doing it. They had a great time together. In the morning at tea break, they would read the daily paper in silence, but doing the dishes they would chat about things to be done around the house and garden. David's father would go outside, line the garbage can with old newspaper, and empty the kitchen bin. Muriel would check the bird feeder in the back garden and maybe remind Fred that the lawn needed cutting. In short, Fred was irreplaceable. I often wished that David would have stepped into the footsteps of his father in his regard as well.

To help me in the kitchen is apparently below David's dignity – he won't even make a second cup of tea! He rarely volunteered for anything but to get the mail, take out the garbage and cut the lawn. He would cut it to perfection like his father. Do I spoil him? Can he blame me? Now that we have moved from our big house up the hill to our small apartment with balcony overlooking the sea, he has an excuse: the kitchen is too small for two. He will sit down for an English breakfast and read the daily paper like a legal document. I have to admit, I too have benefitted from this routine. He reads out to me local and world events which I used to glance over without realizing the implications and thus expanded my horizon. Why should our Senate be abolished? Why does our Prime Minister Harper hesitate? Why does Canadian-born Lord Black want to return to Canada and not live in England where he accepted a Lordship? Indeed, even the news about the European Union and its problems I now read with interest. Lately, he even got up and made us the second cup during breakfast. No, it really does not bother me because my father was the same. Some husbands are domesticated; they even bake bread. I would not like the mess!

Sidmouth, where David aunt, Elsie, and family lived, is nestled between two grand headlands. Because of this protection the seaside resort has a mild climate. Its two beaches are especially suited to safe bathing, sailing and fishing. Here one can enjoy sheltered flowery walks or invigorating rambles over the cliff tops. I asked my photo to be taken when we encountered this thatched house (photo). Elsie's garden was also big and surrounded by high hedges, flowering old trees and lots of flowers. She was lucky to have a gardener. The fishes in her pond were decreasing as they were plucked out by the many seabirds which just flew over the high fences. Nowadays, Sheila, David's cousin, lives in the family home by herself. The maintenance of the old house is a never-ending job, but a real landmark of gracious living.

Getting to know you, getting to know all about you?

When we arrived back at the home of David's parents, his father told us that David's aunt, Sybil, could not see us in the near future. He reminded us that Wimbledon Tennis had started and we should go before we returned to Canada. They even had tickets for us; of course, we could take the car! How very kind of them to let us use the car again. David's father went further to say that he himself had to go up to London to a Directors' meeting. I asked David what his father's business was all about and he replied that he would tell me later, as he had to concentrate on the driving.

David had always found an excuse for not telling me about the business. In 1906 David's grandfather was one of the founders of Freemans, a mail order business, on Clapham Road, in London. The company prospered so much after World War II that they were able to hold their Christmas parties in the Royal Albert Hall. David's father was appointed director, the only one the five directors not related to the founders. Later the British government assisted the business in relocating to an area of high unemployment. Peterborough was north of London. Not surprisingly, none of the directors chose to move from of London to the new location, and changes were coming. When the number of the founders' descendants seeking company shares exceeded fifty, the maximum permitted in a private company, it became necessary to change the company into a public one, and through this some of the founders' children became instant millionaires.

On one of our many camping trips here in Canada, David spoke to a young Englishman who came from the town of Peterborough. He said "Freemans warehouse in Peterborough is no more". The mail order business was bought up by a German outfit which later sold it to Sears which is taking its business away from Peterborough! I was very impressed by the achievements of David's grandfather. In a way, the family reminded me of the Rothschild brothers, who were born in my home town and rose from their humble birth to become famous and powerful by their investments and financial ventures throughout the western world.

Well, by now we were close to Wimbledon and the traffic became heavier. I don't remember how David had found a parking space, but soon we were comfortably seated at Number One court. In 1962 the stadium was much smaller than it is now. Strawberries and cream were already popular and have become now as expensive as the tickets were then. Before the doubles match started we had a surprise. There was a sudden rain shower. Out of nowhere, somebody gave us some plastic covers and we both huddled under them. This was even more exciting for me than the tennis matches we watched later. After more visits to England, I picked up from David's father's commentaries as we watched television together some knowledge of the game. John McEnroe was not among his favourite players, because of his foul language on court. Yet, what an accomplished commentator he has turned out to be!

Getting to know you, getting to know all about you?

While I write of Tennis at Wimbledon I like to insert here another Wimbledon saga. In 1992, Steffi Graf was the darling of the audience. She was about to serve, when a man from the audience stood up and called out in a loud voice: "Steffi will you marry me"? She had heard him. Before she hit the ball she stopped her arm in mid-air and replied: "How much money do you have"? As I was telling the story to the woman next to me at the Vancouver Open Tennis tournament at our country club, she nodded her head and said quietly: "I heard her. I was there. I was playing against her". Her name is Kimiko Date-Krumm. She was seeded #4 in the world, when she was playing against Steffi Graf, who was seeded #1. Steffi married Andre Agassi, another top-ranked player and they "lived happily ever after."

No more tennis talk. Let me go back and talk about theatre plays in London again. "Shock-headed Peter" is based on a German children's tale: *"Der Struwelpeter"* by Dr. Heinrich. I even remember my mother reading it to me. I did not find the production "Monstrously Funny" but the English audience must have liked it, as it had won the Olivier Award in 2002.

Dr. H. Heinrich (1809-1894), physician and reformer of psychiatry, wrote this illustrated book for the children in his care. He was also a citizen of Frankfurt, which had opened a Museum about his collections, when I was visiting my home town in the seventies. To my surprise I was able to order the book here from my favourite bookstore in English. Dear Reader, you will see some the illustrations and headlines printed here. I keep on wondering why I did not like the play "Shock-headed Peter," but fail to come up with an answer.

Earlier on, I reported on the ancient Hadrian's Wall. Not so long ago, on August 13, 1961 a wall was erected to divide the German people during the Cold War. In August 2001 a Vancouver Sun newspaper reporter traced the route of the Berlin Wall, which is now a green strip, and this is what he had to say:

"The barbed wire and the armed border guards with their icy stares and snapping dogs are gone, swept away by the peaceful revolution in 1989. Yet the path of the four meter high Wall can still be found. Researchers say that as many as 238 people died in attempting to escape over the Wall. 3,000 people arrested, an estimated 5,000 successfully entered West Berlin from the East. Now the narrow roadway previously used by East German guards serves as an ideal trail for those in search of fitness, nature, history or a place to walk their dogs. In the inner city it is difficult to track the former border. The Wall made no stop before streets, cemeteries, or underground or tracks. The East German authorities tore down buildings and churches for the Wall, built to stop a flood of emigration, although they said it was a bulwark against Western infiltration".

Christa Wolf, an East German writer, wrote a novel about two lovers which were separated by the Wall: *"Der Geteilte Himmel"* (The Divided Heaven) "Was bleibt?" (What is there left?) In it she reveals she was watched by the State Security Police outside her house during the time of the German Democratic Republic. The English spy writer John Le Carre features the Berlin Wall in his novel "The Spy who came in from the Cold.) On the last page of his book, the hero and his female companion were shot dead while they were climbing the Wall in the darkness of the night. It was not a happy ending.

The photo of the *Potzdamer Platz* in Berlin taken before the Wall came down. If you look carefully, dear Reader, you see that at the top of the gate, the chariot with the horses is looking to the East; whereas it used to look to the West before the Wall came up. Also enclosed, is a postcard showing a jubilant crowd on November 9, 1989 before on the *Brandenburg Platz.*

I was sad to read that there is a certain "nostalgia" occurring in the former German Democratic Republic (GDR) for the good old days. From the tiny broad-hatted walking man (A*mpelmaennchen*) at East German stoplights throughout the country to the long running GDR children's TV show *Sandmann* (Sandman), East German is retro-cool. And certainly there are thing to miss about the old area, said someone. A reporter from the *Globe and Mail,* May 19, 2013, was reviewing hotels under the heading: "One-of-a-kind, three different ways". These converted European hotels blend old and new experiences you won't find anywhere else. There was even an old smoke-spewing boxy Trabant East German-built car in the parking lot of the Berlin hotel.

Yes, there is a Wall in the Brothers Grimm's *Fairy Tales* as well; it is not built of stones or bricks, but of thorns. *Dornroesschen* (The Sleeping Beauty) is one of the better known Children's Tales. I have an edition from the seventies from which I had read to my children. On the enclosed illustration you see the wise women pronouncing their gifts to the newly born princess. Yet the twelfth, who had not been invited to the celebration because there were only eleven golden spoons to be found, appears on the scene. "In the fifteenth year of her age the princess shall prick herself with a spindle and shall fall down dead." Everybody was horrified. Luckily, the eleventh fairy had not yet bestowed her blessings on the baby. She was able to soften this bad

Getting to know you, getting to know all about you?

prediction: "the princess shall not die but fall into a deep sleep for a hundred years." It happened as had been prophesied by the bad fairy and the good fairies.

Many years later, the king's son was passing and he heard from an old man that behind the high thorn hedge there was a castle with a very beautiful princess in it. The curious prince was not to be discouraged and by luck, the one hundred years had just ended. He did not get stuck in the thorns and found his way into the castle were all were asleep. He located the beautiful Rosamund and as he gazed at her, fell in love with her. He bent down to kiss her when she opened her eyes. At the same time, the King and his wife and all the staff in the castle woke up from their 100-year sleep and went on with their work. The Prince took *Dornroesschen* home to his kingdom "where they lived happily ever after" (Sterling, New York & London).

I had better go back to reality! David and I actually visited Berlin while the Wall was up and again after the Wall came down. David agrees with me that the people in the Eastern Zone of Berlin and former East Germany acted differently from the citizens of West Germany. It seemed to us that the older generation could not shake off the prison mentality that the years under the Communist regime had created. However, the younger generation was already more spontaneous and open; they tuned into our conversations easily and looked into our eyes.

We finally said good-bye to David's parents, who promised to visit us. We took the plane to New York to pick up our car. It turned out to be a very hot drive across the States as our air-conditioning broke down, but we made it. Back in Vancouver it was difficult to find an apartment to rent as I was by now heavy with the new babe and not welcome. We got into an apartment block where the owner himself had five boys of his own, not far from the place where we had lived before.

My title to this book is from a popular song, so why not finish with another?

Que Sera Sera

When I was a little girl
I asked my mother
What will I be?
Will I be pretty? Will I be rich?
Here's what she said to me
Que Sera Sera

Getting to know you, getting to know all about you?

Now that I have children of my own
They ask me,
what shall I be?
Will I be handsome? Will I be rich?
Here's what I say to each
Que Sera Sera

It was hard work to raise three boys under the age of five on our own but we made it.

David has been reading a book about *Architecture in Victoria*, the capital of B.C. (by Rosemary James Cross: Dear Brutus Publishing Victoria B.C.). Today he turned to me with a smile and said to my amazement: "There are so many things in that book that remind me of my youth." Since he had excused himself before by saying that he had hardly any memory of his early life in England, my journal actually tells very little about him. Dear Reader, so to speak, I now hand him the pen and he will write it down for us.

Gudrun Honig

PART TWO

Chapter 1

When I (David) was born nine days before Christmas 1928, my older brother, Michael, was less than one year old, having been born in the first week of the same year. At my birth my parents had been married for only two years. They lived near my father's parents in a row house in the town of Surbiton, Surrey, just outside of southwest London. There had been a general strike on their wedding day and there was no public transport, so my mother's father had instructed his chauffeur to drive the bride and groom in his car to their honeymoon location, which was Bournemouth on the south coast. My father had married into a wealthy family and he obviously benefitted financially from the marriage. My mother's parents lived in the nearby town of Kingston. Class distinction at that time would normally have kept my parents apart. They both played tennis and this activity may have been what brought them together.

At my birth, my father was an Articled Clerk (apprentice) with a large London firm of Solicitors (lawyers). In those days law students were seldom paid. Perhaps the law firm saw great potential in this man, who had survived unharmed for four years in the mud-filled trenches in France, starting when he was barely 18 years old. On completing his Articles and passing the Solicitors examinations, my father joined a firm of Solicitors in Woolwich, which was in east London, and moved the family to Bromley, Kent, so as to be nearer to his office. He bought a semi-detached house just outside of southeast London and it was only a twenty-minute bus ride from home to work. My parents were now some distance from their parents and had to make new friends. Most of these were members of the local tennis club where they played.

Getting to know you, getting to know all about you?

I still have a scar on my knee from injuring it when I cycled down the house's garden path before I learned to stop without falling off. Because he was older, Michael had no difficulty with the bike. Although I had overtaken Michael in height, he was more agile with the bike. I was thrilled to watch from my bedroom window the lamplighter arrive at dusk on his bicycle carrying a ladder and a stick. He would lean his ladder against the lamp post, and use his stick to increase the flow of gas to brighten the metal gauze inside the glass-sided miniature house at the top of the pole. I was never awake in time to see the lamplighter return at dawn to turn down the lamps.

I was too young for many events to form a permanent impression on me, but I do remember being woken by my parents one night in 1936 to see a glow in the sky about five miles to the west of our home. It was the burning down and complete destruction of Crystal Palace, a glass building that was erected in Hyde Park in Central London for the 1851 World

Exhibition. Both the building and the exhibition were a great success, but the construction had had to be moved away the next year. At its new location at Streatham in south London, it was not popular and suffered from wear and tear for the many years before the fire finally ended its life.

Getting to know you, getting to know all about you?

Near our house there was a brick wall across the residential street. This was to mark the boundary of the counties of London and Kent. The area beyond the wall was one of the few places in London where a large housing estate could be constructed. During the Depression of the 1930's the area, which was called Downham, was filled with new housing. The streets were curved and many identical two-storey row houses were erected with grassy areas near the roads. The housing estate was quite a show-piece. The buildings were all owned by the local government and rented to the occupiers. There were no garages, for few tenants had cars before or during the Second World War. Trams ran from a terminus on one side of the development to an older area on the other side. At the terminus there were overhead wires to carry the electric power to the trams, but when the trams reached the other side of the new housing estate, the overhead wires were discontinued and a middle rail with an underground electric connection was used to supply power. Sometimes I would hear the screeching of the tram wheels on the tracks. I never had the nerve to go alone into Downham.

Chapter 2

My parents decided that Michael and I would receive our education at Dulwich College Preparatory School and then at age thirteen to continue our education at Dulwich College, which was a famous boys Public School to the west of Bromley. (A Public School was fee-paying and so-named, because, in theory, the students were trained for public service. Free schools were run by the local government and called State Schools.) Michael and I were weekly boarders at the Preparatory School and went home at the weekends and for holidays. I was aged ten and had been going to the Preparatory School for only two years when the start of the Second World War seemed imminent.

Getting to know you, getting to know all about you?

In June of 1939 Mr. Leakey, the Headmaster of the preparatory school, sent a message to the parents stating that the school and staff would be re-located to an orchard near Cranbrook, Kent, and that teaching would resume there in August. (Public Schools in England were normally closed until late in September.) On arriving we found that wooden huts were to be used for both classes and sleeping quarters. The dining room was a very large tent. I recall that the cooking facilities were so primitive that we only ate the food because of our hunger. The boys washed the dirty dishes in bowls. Lavatories were without running water. Surprisingly, few boys complained. We were supplied with gas-masks, which had to be carried all the time. Loudspeakers were also set up so that we could all hear important announcements.

On September 1, 1939, a German army invaded Poland and Mr. Chamberlain, the British Prime Minister, stated that unless the Germans withdrew their army from Poland, Britain would declare war against Germany. I recall saying to another boy that I thought it unlikely that there would be a war. Unfortunately, I was wrong and the Second World War started two days later with sirens sounding all around us. There was a mad scramble and eventually everyone was ready for an attack on our field by Germans with poisonous gas. Of course, there was no attack, but it was good training. Naturally, I was scared.

Early in the following year it was clear to everyone that Kent was not a good place for a school. Kent was where the enemy would most likely invade, because it was the nearest part of England to German-occupied France. Also, enemy bombers on their way to London could be shot down over Kent. Fortunately, the headmaster was able to find a hotel for us in North Wales, which was obviously a far safer location. We boarded a train which took us to a village inland in North Wales called Betys-y-Coed (Chapel-in-the-Wood in English). Life in The Royal Oak Hotel was far more pleasant than in an orchard in Kent. The hotel rooms became dormitories and the area above the stables was converted into class-rooms.

There were no playing-fields in Betws-y-Coed, but the masters kept us busy – and healthy – by taking us on hikes. We also cut the lower branches off the young trees in a recently-planted forest, and collected moss for bedding. There was a

Getting to know you, getting to know all about you?

narrow, but high, bridge over the river that ran nearby and some boys enjoyed jumping off the bridge into it, but I didn't have the courage. One day we hiked the steep route all the way to the top of Mount Snowdon, the highest mountain in England and Wales. On reaching the top, I was amazed to find that on the other side a cog-wheel railway ran all the way up to the top.

There was a village church, where we attended services every day, and I remember an event in that church. It related to the organ which was powered by a water pump. While the organist was playing, one of the boys had to pump the water up to provide the necessary power. I liked to let the water level go down so far that there was just enough power to provide the sound. Strange noises came out of the organ when the water level was too low.

Chapter 3

My brother Michael left the school a year before me, because he had reached the age of thirteen. I was sorry when it was my turn to leave Betws-y-Coed, although it rained a lot in the winter in mountainous North Wales. I especially liked Mr. Taylor, the English teacher, through whom I learned my English grammar, and without which I would have later found the learning of Latin and German very difficult.

Yes, the war continued, but it hardly affected us in our remote location. I was not able to see my parents often, because they did not leave London, but having been at boarding schools for so long, I didn't mind. My father did visit us one summer and we enjoyed his company on the sandy beach of Llandudno on the north coast of Wales. Because of the bombing and the risk of an invasion, my parents decided that, for our next school, Dulwich College in south London was out of the question. Instead they chose Berkhamsted School for our continued education. The school is in a town of the same name in Hertfordshire, about 30 miles northwest of London. It seemed a lot further away, because it was surrounded by fields and to the north there were gentle hills.

The town of Berkhamsted has a long history. It is where, in 1066, the English surrendered to William the Conqueror. It has a busy road, four railway tracks and a canal running through the middle of the town. I used to like watching the steam trains rushing by. While I was at school there, one train crashed with the loss of several lives, because it was travelling too fast when switching from one track to another. Some railway employees were on strike and the relief train driver apparently was not watching the signals. The canal was used to carry goods to London on long, narrow motorized boats. During the war there was no fuel for the engines, so horses were brought back to pull the boats. I used to enjoy walking along the tow-path at the edge of the canal, but had to watch that I didn't arrive back at school with horse "dirt" on my shoes. The tow-path was only on one side of the canal and at places there was a narrow foot-bridge with the path continuing on the other side. The horses and pedestrians would use the bridge to cross the canal.

At Berkhamsted School we had to play sports on two or three afternoons a week. The sports fields were on the top of the hill on the other side of town and we had to walk both to and from the fields. There was no choice of sports: it was cricket in the summer term, rugby in the winter term and running in the spring term. At cricket I was scared of the ball hurting my hands or face, so I was not very successful at catching the ball or hitting it with the bat, when it came in my direction. There was very little fuel for the lawn mower, so the grass away from the wickets grew quite long and at times I would lie hidden in the long grass.

Getting to know you, getting to know all about you?

Rugby was also a problem for me, because I couldn't wear my spectacles and, because of my short-sightedness, most of the time I didn't know where the ball was. However, I followed the crowd and was useful in pushing in the scrum, when required. Running was a sport that I could manage, because of my long legs and I am sure it was good for my heart and lungs. I believe that my continued good health is derived from running and later walking. However, running is not a team sport and I wish I had benefited from playing in a team.

There was an indoor swimming pool at the school, but I didn't learn to swim, because most of the time there was neither enough fuel to operate the pumps to draw the water up from the subterranean wells, nor to heat the water. It was not until I was in Canada that I learned to swim, and I still swim regularly. I would have liked to have learned how to play a few more sports, but was not given the chance. I suppose you could say that the training I received in the Officers (later Junior) Training Corps was a sport. We were provided with uniforms left over from the First World War and wooden rifles. We marched in the gravel-covered school quadrangle carrying our lightweight rifles and it must have amused the townsfolk. After the war ended we were allowed to wear Second World War uniforms and fire real rifles at indoor targets. I think I would have been more accurate if I had been permitted to use a left-handed rifle, as I am left-handed.

Many of the regular teachers were away until after the war and we were taught by some men who had come back from retirement. The quality of teaching seemed to me to be uneven, but I suppose the war effort came first. I was never in a school play, was never taught a musical instrument, and I was sorry that I had not the experience of performing in front of others. In those days schooling consisted of sitting at desks lined up in rows and listening to the teacher. Excursions were rare and even then we did not go far from the school. I understand that nowadays students work together and share their knowledge.

The hall, in which we wrote our homework, consisted of four rows of benches with desk tops. The youngest boys sat in the front row and the eldest in the back row. One rule, enforced by the older boys, was that, during evening homework, you were not allowed to speak to or even look at the boys in the rows behind you. From the clock, which was hanging behind the back row, the boys could tell from it when it was their turn for a bath. There were no showers for washing after sports and each boy was assigned a 20-minute period twice a week during evening homework in which to have his bath and return to his seat. I was embarrassed when I returned about 15 minutes late from my first bath. All the boys following me had a lot less than 20 minutes to get to the bathroom, run the water, undress, wash, dry, dress and return to the hall. I soon learned to speed up.

While we were boarding at Berkhamsted School, the war in Western Europe was won by the American armies, with help from soldiers from Britain and many other countries, but nothing changed at school. Britain was almost bankrupt and the government continued to ration food and impose high rates of income tax. At school I never felt I was starving, but I would have liked a greater quantity and variety of food. Those who remembered the problems after the First World War feared a repeat of the same, but this time, thankfully, there was no deadly influenza epidemic and the soldiers did not have to wait long before returning home.

Getting to know you, getting to know all about you?

Chapter 4

When Michael reached the age of 18, he was conscripted into the army for his two years of compulsory military service. I followed a year later. Because both our birthdays were around Christmas, we both stayed at school until December and, so, left in the middle of the school year. There was no graduation ceremony for us and, as far as I know, not one for anyone else. We had both passed our School Certificate examinations, but had not attempted a higher level. At that time we could study either Latin or Geography. I had studied Latin, but had not passed the examination. I preferred Geography to Latin, so switched courses for the last year of school and it turned out to be my favourite subject.

Gudrun Honig

I had to report to an army base in the first week of January, 1947, and was given the number 19136324 with demobilisation group number 104. I had no difficulty adjusting to life in the army, but some of the boys were homesick, as this was the first time they had been away from home. Also my experience with the Junior Training Corps at school was a help with uniform care and constant marching. I was at a camp near Maidstone in Kent for the first six weeks. That winter was an unusually cold one and it snowed while I was there. The sergeant of my platoon was a supporter of the local football (soccer) team and arranged for the whole platoon to "volunteer" to shovel away some of the snow from the sports field. That was my introduction to the ways of the army and I was careful after that never to volunteer for any tasks. Potential leaders always volunteer and I realise now that I showed lack of initiative to my army superiors by not offering to help.

From Maidstone I was transferred to the barracks in Aldershot for assessment. Almost all of the new soldiers had had jobs after leaving school at age 16, but I had continued at school until I was "called up". The officer, who selected the occupation of the soldiers for the next two years, gave me various tests and decided that, unlike many young soldiers, I would survive for a long period sitting in a classroom. I was, therefore, transferred to some barracks at an unused airfield in Yorkshire in the north of England, where I was taught to be a Radio Mechanic. Radios were made differently in those days: valves and resistors were necessary parts. A valve had a glass cover and pins underneath. Like light bulbs used until recently in homes, the valve had to be replaced from time to time. The strength of a resistor was measured by the various coloured stripes near one end. Each colour denoted a number. The whole thing was quite complicated and it was not surprising that the course was eight months long and only those who came straight from school

Getting to know you, getting to know all about you?

could survive sitting in a classroom that long. By the time I left the army, both valves and resistors were obsolete!

During one weekend, while I was in Yorkshire, I hitch-hiked to the Lake District. I wore my uniform and pick-ups were easy. On another occasion I hitched to the town of Whitby on the nearby Yorkshire coast. At a fairground there I was very impressed by a man "swallowing" a sword. Whitby was certainly a much poorer place than any town I had seen on the south coast of England. I thought it enterprising of me to make these excursions on my own. On completing the course, I was given a badge and a distinctive beret and sent to Liverpool to catch a military ship sailing to Tobruk near Egypt. The town is best remembered as the place where the Allies stopped the Germans from advancing in Egypt.

Gudrun Honig

Getting to know you, getting to know all about you?

Chapter 5

The vessel I sailed in from Liverpool was a converted cargo ship and I remember that one soldier in my group was sick even before the ship left the dock! This was my first and only experience of sleeping in a hammock. The rough sea in the Bay of Biscay was not pleasant, but I enjoyed the calm Mediterranean Sea. We dis-embarked on the south side of the Mediterranean Sea at Tobruk. There were many sunken ships in the harbour, and masts and funnels seemed to be sticking up everywhere. From there it was a long bumpy lorry ride along the coastal road back to Bengazi and then inland to Barce, where I was going to remain for a year. At one time on the journey the water in the engine of our truck was getting low, so the soldiers helped out!

We were stationed near the village of Barce in a very pleasant former Italian hospital and slept in the single-storey dormitories. The Italians had colonised the country of Libya before the war and fascist signs and Italian words still appeared on some of the whitewashed building walls, although the war had ended there three years before we arrived. After the war ended, the Americans occupied the western part of Libya, by then called Tunisia. British troops were in Cyrenaica in the east with Bengazi as its capital. I was very interested to see that the people in the fields around us lived in tents and they put their goats in small houses that had presumably been built by the Italians for the people to occupy. I had never seen poverty like this – the people had nothing! There was a steady supply of electricity for us, which I learned was from a power station run by German prisoners-of-war. I do not know whether the Germans were waiting to be released or if they had chosen to remain there. Before I left Barce, a German sold me a jewel box made of aluminium from a shot-down aeroplane with "Bengazi, 1949" scratched on it. It has stood the test of time and is one of my oldest and dearest souvenirs.

My training to be a radio mechanic was of little use, because it was so much easier to replace a radio than to repair it, unless the failed component was a tube. Each tube had a set of metal pins to connect it to the set, and it was not difficult to remove a tube that did not light up and replace it with a new one. I was attached to a group of soldiers whose equipment was small armoured cars, each of which required a radio. Occasionally the whole unit would march through the village as a show of force. All the soldiers wore black berets, but mine was khaki, as I was not part of the unit. I certainly felt the odd man out in my khaki beret.

One weekend I took the bus from Barce to the large town of Bengazi on the coast. I bought some ground-nuts, also called pea-nuts or monkey-nuts, from a street trader. Afterwards I was violently sick and I did not touch any nuts for years afterwards. In the summer we were sometimes driven to a beach nearer than Bengazi. We were warned that the summer sun would burn exposed skin, but our sergeant thought he knew better; as a result, his back was so badly burned that he could hardly bear to wear a shirt and removed it whenever possible. Getting sunburnt was an offence in the army, so he could not go to the sick bay for treatment, and he really suffered. Another outing was to what was called "Cleopatra's Pool". It was a large pool on the water's edge hewn out of solid rock and it must have been a very laborious undertaking. I learned afterwards that the pool was indeed carved in Cleopatra's time.

Getting to know you, getting to know all about you?

Chapter 6

Eventually, after a year in Africa, my demobilisation group (number 104) reached the top of the list and I was trucked to Tunis and shipped from there to England. On the way home, the ship stopped at Gibraltar, where the trusting locals sent goods up to the railing on strings in the hope of receiving cash in return. I think I should have used my two years in the army more profitably, but at that stage in my life, I had not learned to lead – only to follow.

Back home I saw again the air-raid shelter that had been dug for my parents into the slope at the side of the tennis court. We had slept in the shelter during the latter part of the war, when we were on holiday from Berkhamsted School. Although there was no longer any risk of invasion by the Germans, attacks on London from the air continued with bombers, then with unmanned planes, called Flying Bombs or V-1s, and finally with rockets, called V-2s. Launching of the rockets continued until early 1945, when all of the launching pads on the continent had finally been captured by Allied troops. No defence to V-2 rockets was possible and no air-raid shelter was safe from the large bomb they carried. They did the most damage, but like the V-1s, the V-2s were not accurate enough to hit any definite target. Fortunately, no bomb of any kind fell near our house, although parts of exploded British anti-aircraft shells broke some tiles.

After demobilisation I enjoyed life with my parents and my friends, but I was delayed in starting my five-year "Articles" (apprenticeship), as the English Law Society required me to pass the Latin examination in the School Certificate. After some private tuition, I passed the examination and started work at my father's small City of London law office. Being in the City, I was able to learn something of the area. There was even a Roman Temple buried nearby. Thanks to the efficient railway system, the journey to work was no problem. However, the office only prepared mortgages of land, releases of mortgages and handled the funds. Each transaction was done at a lawyer's office by exchanging a bank draft for the title documents. My father was not at all pleased when I told him that one day on the way to a law office at a coastal resort I had had a swim in the sea and had left my clothes on the beach with the bank draft in a pocket. I especially enjoyed the company of one of the secretaries, but after she came in one day and showed everyone the new engagement ring her boyfriend had given her, I kept my distance.

After I passed the Solicitor's Intermediate Examination, my apprenticeship was transferred to a solicitor in Bromley. This enabled me to learn about other aspects of a law office and I occasionally went into London to appear before a Master in the High Court. My boss's name was Edward ("Teddy") Hessenberg and I used to admire his acting in plays at the local theatre. One summer he was late returning from his holidays and I was told it was because of lack of wind in the English Channel, where he had

Getting to know you, getting to know all about you?

been sailing. He told me I should be taking days off to "go to the horse races," but I suppose I was not mature enough by then to venture away from the office.

The tennis court in our garden looked good, but it did not get much use. The white lines had to be marked out each week after the grass was cut. The distance between the service line and the neighbour's fence was too short, and the balls would keep going over the fence. More importantly, my friends were two miles away at Bromley Cricket Club and transportation was not easy. In the summer I played a lot of tennis at the Club, but my backhand was never good enough. At first I used to cycle both ways, but later Michael passed on to me my mother's pre-war 2-seater convertible. It weighed so little that, when the battery was low, I was able to push the car to start the engine. Sometimes I used the crank handle.

Gudrun Honig

On Saturday evenings I often went to a public dance with a group of my tennis friends and, surprisingly, no one refused to dance with me, although I couldn't keep in step with the music. Most of the activities of the tennis group were done as a group, but I also took girls individually to dinner or to a play in London. However, I never felt I wanted to have any of the girls as a permanent girl-friend – one with whom I would like to spend my life. Although several of the young men and women did inter-marry, I couldn't see myself stuck in that group for the rest of my life.

I once spent a very enjoyable fortnight on the Norfolk Broads in Eastern England on a sailing boat with three other people. We sailed all day, moored it in the evening and slept on the boat at night. The girls did the cooking. I don't remember if the boys did any work. I liked Alan Marks and Leslie West the best. They later married and they are the only English friends I still write to. I once arranged to go hiking with Alan. I said I would carry a small suitcase, but he explained that a rucksack would be easier to carry. I certainly had a lot to learn. Later we took a hiking holiday together in the Dolomites, which are mountains in northern Italy.

Getting to know you, getting to know all about you?

This meant carrying spare clothing, some food and some bedding. Alan and I walked each day from one Youth Hostel building to another and we covered quite a distance. Very enjoyable!

A friend, who was also about to qualify as a lawyer, said he assumed that on passing his examinations, he would obtain a position in a lawyer's office, find a wife, buy a house and settle down. I didn't think I was ready for that sort of thing and looked into the prospect of travelling for a while. I needed to work while travelling and discovered there were not many parts of the world where I could use my knowledge of English law. Alan Marks said he had a friend who had worked at a logging camp in British Columbia (B.C.) in Western Canada. I found out that the south coast of B.C. had a very similar climate to that of England. In 1848 (the year it became a British colony) B.C. adopted the civil laws of England. Naturally, necessary changes had been made to bring the laws up-to-date. I thought I would start my travels in Vancouver and that if I lived there I could sail and hike in the summer and ski in the winter. I also had a cousin living in B.C. who could help me. I wrote to the Law Society of B.C. and they confirmed that a lawyer from England could practice as a Barrister and Solicitor in B.C. after being employed by a B.C. lawyer for one a half years and passing the necessary examinations.

However, I needed to pass the English Law Society's Final Examination, which I had failed on my first attempt. While attending extra classes in London, I booked a passage on a ship to Canada and on a train across Canada to Vancouver. I re-wrote the examination and thought that I had again answered the questions poorly, so went to the travel agents again and asked them to cancel the reservation. They talked me into postponing my decision. I did indeed pass the examination and was

Gudrun Honig

appointed a Solicitor of the Supreme Court of England. When I told by parents of my decision to go travelling, they were, naturally, very disappointed. My father said he could help me to get into a good law firm in England, but not elsewhere. It was hard for me to go away against my parents' wishes, but I said that it was only to go travelling, which what I thought at the time. This idea of travelling alone to Canada and living there for a while was certainly a sign of my new independence.

Getting to know you, getting to know all about you?

<u>Chapter 7</u>

I arrived in Vancouver on June 1, 1957, and thought everything was wonderful. In my second week in Vancouver I hiked from Downtown through Stanley Park, across Lions Gate Bridge and up Grouse Mountain to the top of the gondola. Then I hiked down again and back to Vancouver. Of course, I was very tired that night, but I thought it wonderful to have accessible high mountains that were so close to the city.

I quickly secured a position with a lawyer in downtown Vancouver and was paid $125 a month. That was a very small amount, but I found accommodation, with some meals included, for $85 a month. I soon realized I could not get anywhere without a car, so I invested $300 in a used car. I spent a further $150 on driving lessons, car repairs and insurance for the car, and that was almost the end of my worldly savings.

After a month in Vancouver, I resolved to visit my cousin, Claude, and his wife, Florence. They lived in central B.C. in the town of Prince George about 400 miles north of Vancouver (about 500 miles by road). I took the Greyhound bus and was scared when the bus driver took the bus up the Fraser Canyon. The cliffs were so steep and the road so narrow and winding, it seemed that we could never get around the next corner safely. However, the driver kept going and I arrived safely in Prince George. When I told Claude that I had given up my seat for part of the journey, because there were native women standing, he said I should not have stood up for them. I said I was not used to that racial discrimination and felt that I had done the right thing. My impression of Prince George was that the town existed only because it was a convenient place to saw trees into wood for housing. There were several sawmills on the edge of town. Because the roads break up in the very cold winters, few of the roads had any surface other than gravel. The snow had just melted and dandelions were flowering everywhere. I was glad I had not chosen Prince George for my future residence. I have not been back.

Later, I went to Winnipeg, Manitoba (about 1,200 miles east of Vancouver) for a few days to visit my uncle Vernon in Dauphin and another uncle's daughter in Morden. After the First World War, two of my mother's brothers had migrated from England to these places. The uncle who lived in Morden (about 50 miles southwest of Winnipeg and near the U.S. border) had several children and died before I went to Canada. I visited one of his daughters. Her husband had contracted polio on a visit to Iceland, his country of origin, and lived by being connected to an iron lung, but was somehow able to continue being a school teacher. I still exchange Christmas cards with the daughter and had thought of visiting again, but the summers are too hot for me, the winters too cold for me and the stories of mosquitoes around Winnipeg are alone enough to stop me going to Manitoba.

In the small rural town of Dauphin (about 150 miles northwest of Winnipeg) my uncle Vernon showed me the first house he had had built and, nearby, his present house with a large open air swimming pool. He suggested we look at his cattle and, to my amazement we got into a jeep and drove me around a huge area while he tried to count the cattle, some of which were out of sight. I had not realised that due to the hot summers and cold winters, grass grew for only a short time in the year: very large fields were required to feed the cattle in the summer and supply fodder for the winter. For half of the year the cattle were in barns. In England the fields are small, the cattle are outside all day and there is enough grass for them to enjoy all year round.

Getting to know you, getting to know all about you?

Chapter 8
Because I had qualified as an English solicitor, I was one of the few who could become a B.C. lawyer without having to get a university undergraduate degree and a law degree. In my Vancouver law office I was never busy and was able to use office time to read some statutes in preparation for the required written and oral examinations. In preparing for examinations in England I was able to read books that explained the law, but there were few legal textbooks dealing with B.C. law. I passed the B.C. written examination and the short oral one that followed. I was then a B.C. solicitor. I practiced law for one year and automatically become a B.C. barrister. By January, 1957, eighteen months after arriving in B.C., I was, therefore, a fully qualified B.C. lawyer. It seems an easy way to become a lawyer, but I had worked and studied in England for more than five years before coming to Canada.

The lawyer who employed me had two problems with which I had no experience. One was that he was drinking in his office. Some afternoons he was not fit enough to see clients, so appointments were made for the morning only. His other problem related to his secretary-bookkeeper, whom he fired after he found out that, when clients paid cash for work done, she gave them receipts and then deposited smaller sums into the lawyer's bank account. The secretary kept the difference. These experiences on my first job in Canada were not things that I had studied or learned about in England, and I was shocked.

Chapter 9
When I was not in the office, I had a very busy social life. I played tennis some evenings and went out for dinner, theatre or cinema on other evenings – never alone. I joined the Canadian Youth Hostel Association and went to their weekly meetings. At the meetings people signed up for outings. In the summer and until

Gudrun Honig

October we would hike up mountains as a group, but there was too much snow on the ground in the winter and spring, so the group would stay near sea level except for a few skiing or snow-shoeing trips. My first big hike was to the top of 10,000 ft. Mount Baker in Washington State. Near the peak we had to cross crevasses in the ice and for that a pick-axe and a rope were required. With help from experienced climbers, I managed to reach the top, from where I could smell the sulphur coming from cracks in the almost-extinct volcano, but clouds completely blocked the view. I did not use the pick-axe again for climbing, but found it very useful later for digging in the garden.

In October 1959, I drove to Mexico with four other Youth Hostellers. One of the men was Colin, with whom I was sharing an apartment. He was an architect and came from my part of England. The other man, Ashley, was an Australian and an organiser. One "girl", Dorothy, was from Scotland, and the other, Judy, was from New Zealand. I liked both girls. We bought a used car and filled the roof-rack and trunk with food and spare clothing. The girls always sat in the back with one of the men and neither girl complained about the squeeze or having to do all the cooking. We tried to visit all the interesting places in the U.S. Rockies and west to the coast by zigzagging around. San Francisco, Los Angeles, San Diego, Salt Lake City, Yellowstone National Park, Bryce Canyon, Grand Canyon, Las Vegas and Death Valley were places we visited and tented nearby. After camping on the north edge of Grand Canyon, Colin drove the car to the south side, while the rest of us walked down to the river where we slept in an empty hut, then crossed at the bridge and hiked all the way up the other side to the tourist area, where Colin waited for us in the car. It was an exhausting hike and one that few people do, but I am proud that I did it. The whole adventure from Vancouver to Mexico was certainly a wonderful experience and far more interesting than I expected

Getting to know you, getting to know all about you?

After seeing much of Western United States, Colin left us at the Mexican border to make his way to England and we continued driving south all the way to Mexico City. On the way back to U.S.A., I crashed the car and we were lucky that no one was seriously injured. I broke some teeth and a couple of ribs and still have bumps on my head. We were not wearing seat belts and I probably did the damage to myself on the steering wheel. The others flew back to Vancouver, while I flew to Texas to visit a cousin I had never seen and then to Denver to visit another cousin whom I had seen in England many years earlier. They were children of another of Mother's sisters, who had migrated to the U.S.A. before World War II. Back in Vancouver I found a job with a trust company, which paid me more than I could get at a law firm.

Chapter 10

I decided that it was not wise to continue with the Youth Hostel group. They were mostly from Britain, Australia or New Zealand, and had no intention of settling in Vancouver. They all had plans to move on, while I wanted to be among those who were making

Gudrun Honig

Vancouver their permanent home. However, I had met and was friendly with Michael, a lawyer from England, who had also qualified as a B.C. lawyer. He was living in Vancouver with his girl-friend, Janet, who came with him from England. Michael could not find suitable employment in Vancouver and decided to move up to the small town of Burns Lake, some distance west of Prince George. Janet refused to go there with him.

Janet had to find a place to live in Vancouver. Michael asked me to look after Janet, while they were separated. In the lawyer's office, where she worked, there was another legal secretary, who wanted to share accommodation. I found myself helping both Janet and the other legal secretary move their belongings up the steep stairs to their rooms in the old house, which they had chosen as their home. On the stairs I met Gudrun (who calls herself "Gudy"), and it was my lucky day. She was from Germany and different from the English women I had known. We soon fell in love and, after a few months, at the end of 1960, we married and both of us started a new life. I was no longer alone, but instead was able to experience life with a girl I loved. I was a different person.

Made in the USA
Charleston, SC
13 September 2015